Joseph Price

A second letter to the Right Honourable Edmund Burke

Joseph Price

A second letter to the Right Honourable Edmund Burke

ISBN/EAN: 9783337150440

Printed in Europe, USA, Canada, Australia, Japan

Cover: Foto ©ninafisch / pixelio.de

More available books at **www.hansebooks.com**

LETTER

To the Right Honourable

EDMUND BURKE, Esq;

On the Subject of the Evidence referred to in the Second Report of the SELECT COMMITTEE of the House of Commons, appointed to enquire into the State of Justice in the Provinces of Bengal, Bahar, and Orressa.

With a compleat refutation of every Paragraph of the Letter of Mr. Philip Francis, to the Court of Directors of the East India Company, copied from No. 7, of the Appendix to the said Report,

---

Printed for the Author, and sold by the Booksellers of London and Westminster.

MDCCLXXXII.

A

SECOND LETTER

To EDMUND BURKE. *Esq.*

SIR,

SINCE the publication of my letter to you, on the subject of the execution of Rajah Nundcomar, I have been asked in what part of the former report of the committee, it appeared in evidence that it was by many persons at Bengal, believed that the Rajah lost his life on political principles, for that it was not to be found in page 59 of the former report as referred to in my quotation from the latter.

This information set me to examine the first report, and I find that the only parts in it where this circumstance is mentioned is in page 57 and page 58, as printed by J. Evans, No. 32, Paternoster-Row.

This re-examination of the fact, and of the authority, has opened a new scene of investigation, the developing of which

which, will ſhew very plainly on what ſlight grounds, and for what particular purpoſe the inſinuations have been taken up, and brought forward in the laſt report.

I have been told and otherways informed, that my eagerneſs to vindicate the Governor General of Bengal, together with the warmth of my temper, had hurried me into ſome perſonalities which had obſcured my agreement, and weakened it very much.

This remark having its foundation in truth has hurt me a good deal, not on account of the men themſelves, but that a good cauſe ſhould be hurt by an injudicious advocate. But as I have yet abundant materials unapplied, I once more take the liberty to addreſs you on the ſubject; by keeping to facts and argument and leaving men to their own feelings, I hope to reclaim all the moderate to my ſide of the queſtion.

The preſent report refers to the laſt for the evidence, which the committee deſires may be applied to, in juſtification of their new doctrine of policy.—To that let us go, and fairly ſtate the grounds they have gone upon, to the application of which I have ſo ſtrongly objected.

The cauſes of the tryal, condemnation, and execution of the Rajah Nundcomar, being part of the duty of the committee, it appears that ſeven different gentlemen were called before them to be examined on that head: the two firſt were members of the committee, Meſſrs. Rouſe and Farrer. Mr. Mills and Mr. Price, two very old Free Merchants, who had reſided many years in Bengal. Mr. Baber, a company's ſervant, and one of the provincial Revenue Chiefs, Major James Rennell, the company's ſurveyor

ſurveyor general, and Capt. Cowe, a military officer in the company's army.

The firſt five give their evidence clear and diſtinct, all agreeing in the ſame points, that the Rajah's ſuffering ſo ignominious a death ſurpriſed the people much, as it was contrary to their ideas of juſtice, that a man of his rank and high caſt of religion ſhould ſuffer capitally for what they deemed a venal offence. Not one ſingle word is ſaid about political influence, by any one of the firſt ſix gentlemen, nor does it appear that Capt. Cowe had ſuch an idea in his head, untill it had been introduced there by the Novel, and ſingular queſtion put to him by ſome one member of the committee.

The fair way is to give his evidence at length, and to reaſon on the ſingularity of it afterwards.

I have taken it from J. Evans's publication, page 57 and 58, it is as follows:

" Capt. Cowe being again examined by your committee, " was aſked whether he was at Calcutta at the time of " the proceedings againſt Nundcomar; and at the time " of his execution, ſaid he was, during the whole of the " time, being aſked. if any criminal proſecution had been " commenced againſt him before that indictment for " forgery? he ſaid none that he had heard of. Being " aſked, what was the opinion of the natives concern- " ing that proceeding, whether they thought it political, " or done in the ordinary courſe of juſtice. Said, he be- " lieved there was a great diverſity of opinions; that " many thought it was done from political motives.—— " Others in the ordinary courſe of juſtice, according to the

" the laws of England, being asked, what was the cha-
" racter of the Rajah Nundcomar among the natives?
" Said, that he was considered at a man of understand-
" ing, but much adicted to letigation, and in general
" thought a designing artful man; that he never heard
" any thing farther against his moral character. Being
" asked, whether his prosecution did not give general
" satisfaction to the natives, as being the means of bring-
" ing to justice a criminal, who had been a long time
" protected from it by his power and artifices? Said,
" he never heard that it had given satisfaction, except
" to few, who might have viewed it in a political light.
" Being asked, whether he had not heard that the offence
" for which Nundcomar was tried, was committed several
" years before the trial? He said, he always understood
" it had been committed for many years before the trial.
" Being asked, if he had an opportunity to make any
" observations concerning the execution of Nundcomar?
" Said he had, that he saw the whole, except the imme-
" diate act of execution. From the parapet of the new
" fort, not quite half a mile from the place of execution,
" there were eight or ten thousand people assembled; who
" at the moment the Rajah was turned off, dispersed sud-
" denly crying, Ah-Baup-aree, leaving nobody about the
" gallows but the sheriff and his attendance, and a few
" European spectators. He explains the term of Ah-Baup-
" aree, to be an exclamation of the black people, upon
" the appearance of any thing very alarming, and when
" they are in great pain: that they did not think he would
" be put to death till he was actually executed. That
" many of them even ran into the river, from the terror
" at seeing a Bramin executed in that ignominious manner.
" That the circumstance of his execution was received
" with great horror by all the natives, as well as most

of

" of the Europeans; who, in general, thought it a hard " cafe. Being afked, if the natives in general were not " fatisfied with the introduction of the rigor of the " Englifh penal ftatute law, as tending to fecure credit " and fidelity in dealings? Said, as far as he ever under- " ftood, quite the reverfe.——Then being afked, whe- " ther equity and impartiality of the fupreme court in that " bufinefs, did not ftrike forcibly upon the minds of the " natives, and imprefs them with a ftrong idea of the " wifdom and juftice of the Englifh laws, and a defire " of having them extended for the general benefit? He " informed your committee, that it rather impreffed " them with an unfavourable idea of our juftice and " equity; and that he never heard they, by any means, " wifhed to have them extended. Being afked, if the " natives knew for what purpofe the fupreme court had " been eftablifhed? He faid, he believed at firft they did " not properly underftand it, but that by this time, they " are perfectly acquainted with the nature of its inftitution. " Being afked, if it was not generally given out, that " this court was inftituted for their protection and their " defence, againft the abufes of European authority? He " faid, it was, that he remembered hearing Mr. Le Maiftre, " one of the judges from the bench, exprefs'd his furprife, " that fo many people applied for redrefs to the country " courts, when they might depend upon as good juftice " or better, in the fupreme court of judicature; and that " thefe were his very words. Being afked, if the natives " confidered the proceedings againft Nundcomar, and his " execution, as anfwering the ends of the inftitution of " the court in the protection of the natives? He faid, " he did not believe they did. Being afked, whether they " did not confider the execution, as having a tendency to " encourage them to prefer complaints againft Europeans

in

" in authority? He said he believed not. Being asked, " whether an address to the judges was not signed by seve- " ral of the natives, commending their conduct in the " office, and particularly dwelling upon the character of " mercy? He said, that he has seen an address from the " Armenian merchants, printed, which, he believes was " given to the judges. Being asked, whether that address " contradicted the sentiments of the natives, which he " had just now mentioned? He said it did. Then being " asked, whether he looked upon that address, or the con- " versation he had heard, as most truly expressive of the " genuine sense of the natives? He said, he believed the " conversation he had heard, to be the most expressive; " and that the address does by no means express their " sense. Being asked, if he recollected any instance of " mercy, to which that address alluded? He said none, " except the release of the felons, and several who had " been under sentence of death in the prison at Calcutta " for capital offences. Then being asked, if any particular " circumstances of hardship had been represented to the " judges? he said, he did not know that there had, be- " fore the arrival of the judges. And being asked, whe- " ther an opinion had prevailed, that the construction or " execution of criminal law had been severe and immo- " derate? he said, he never had heard any such opinion."

Messrs. Rous, Farrer, Mills, Price and Rennell, had been examined before, Capt. Cowe, and Mr. Baber was examined after him, not one of the other gentlemen mentioned a syllable of policy, or hinted that such an idea had ever been conceived. Capt. Cowe was going on, in the same line. When he was asked by some one of the gentlemen of the committee, " What was the opinion of the

" natives

" natives concerning that proceeding, whether they thought " it political or done in the ordinary courſe of juſtice."

I have read the whole report over and over, to find out if it was poſſible what could give cauſe for ſuch a queſtion, no ſuch had been put to any one of the proceeding five evidence, nor to the one which followed, and candour obliges me to conclude, that, it was not the effect of deſign, but meer matter of accident. The anſwer goes to declare what was very true, that party diviſions, in the ſettlement had begot different opinions, in the inhabitants, but not the leaſt inference can be drawn from Capt. Cowe's evidence, that this ſuppoſed political interpoſition, applied to any particular deſcription of men, either to the judges, the majority of the civil government, or to the minority.

The exclamation Au-Baup-a-ree, and the ſaying the people run into the river on the Rajah's being turned off, conveyes improper notions to the mind of the reader, and in candour they ought to have been explained why the gentlemen of the committee, who underſtand the Hindoo manners and cuſtoms did not do it, I will not truſt myſelf to ſay for fear I ſhould again touch ſore places ; but the fact is as follows : had a calf been knocked on the head they would have done the ſame ; the exclamation cannot be rendered into Engliſh, the idioms of the languages is ſo very different ; but if an Hindoo was to ſee a houſe on fire ; to receive a ſmart ſlap on the face ; break a China baſon ; cut his finger ; ſee two Europeans boxing, or a ſparrow ſhot, he would call out Au-Baup-aree.

When the Rajah was hanged, it was to them a very extraordinary ſight, and it was natural for Hindoos to ſuppoſe, that it in ſome degree defiled them. The remedy was at hand, near to the gallows where the Rajah ſuffered, runs a branch of the river Ganges, the waters of which river, in the ideas of all the Hindoo nations, cleanſe them from every kind of impurity. Had a common pickpocket ſuffered; had a European ſpit by accident on the outer edge of their outer garment; had they touched any dead animal, or fifty thouſand other the moſt trifling cauſes would have induced them to go and purify themſelves in the Ganges. At all hours of day and night, at all ſeaſons of the year thouſands of them are ſeen, men, women and children mingled together, indiſcriminately dabling in the river to purge away the impurities of body, ſoul, and garment, at the ſame inſtant, and by the ſame means.

With ſuch an explanation as this I have given, (and I have with me, the unanimous opinions of all the authors, who have written on, and of every man in this kingdom who knows the leaſt of the manners and cuſtoms of the Hindoos.) How ridiculous does the above diſmal ſtory of Capt. Cowes appear; and how ſhall we account for five or ſix members of the committee, giving up ſuch cock and bull accounts, to terrify our women and children, it can do no more, for ſurely no man of the leaſt intelligence can ſuppoſe the people run into the river from terror and diſmay, not they truly. Hanging a Bramin was a novelty to be ſure, but if five hundred ſuch raſcally Bramins as Maha Rajah Nundcomar had ſuffered the ſame death, not

not an Hindoo among them would have gone without his dinner on the occaſion.

They are by no means a ſanguinary ſet of people, their religion teaches them, not to take away the life of a fly wantonly, nor will they do it, this in many inſtances, they carry to what we ſhould call a ridiculous extreme. Yet theſe people have laws among them, which would ſhock the moſt hardened Europeans. They impale alive wretches who have twice been detected in robbing in boats on the river: they ſcourge to death for theft, and they mutilate, by cutting of the hand, the ears, or the noſe, for houſe-breaking or robberies on the road. Nothing can be ſo erroneous, or liable to miſlead the judgment ſo much as comparing ſome few particular laws and cuſtoms of one country, with a few of thoſe of another. The Hindoos, would no more change their own code, ſuch as it is, with Engliſhmen, then Engliſhmen would change with them. Their's ſuit beſt with their climate, is interwoven with their religion, and they have been poſſeſſed of it ages before the people of this kingdom knew whether they dwelt on an iſland, or on the continent.

But to return to our ſubject, this ſingle evidence of Capt. Cowe, which grew out of the oddity of the queſtion, without which it never would have entered his head, to have amuſed the committee with ſuch an idle tale, of whimſical political interference; nor do I believe that it was more thought of by any one member of the committee, otherwiſe when the Bengal judicial bill was introduced into the

House of Commons, how came it to pass without any mention having been made, or even a hint started that it would be improper to leave in possession of the civil and judicial powers at Calcutta, monsters, who had been guilty of such an infamous conspiracy. All the public evidence that has been yet produced was known then: If there is private information it ought not to be held back from the public eye. If it is held back, and either the judges or Governor-general Hastings suffer in the mind of one single fellow subject, male or female, from the inferences held up in the report of the committee. It is a mode of punishment, unknown to the laws of the land, and not to be justified on any principles but such as are adopted at the inquisition, and no man can say whose turn it shall come to next, to have his honour arraigned. There is another committee, who deal more candidly, facts are produced and the supposed culprit is candidly informed that attempts will openly and fairly be made to fix criminality upon him, but that every assistance will be given him to defend himself, and no advantage taken of popular clamour to prejudice his cause; had I a brother in such a situation, sharp as the fraternal feelings might pierce my soul, I should bow to the ground in reverence to the justice of my country. I would sooth him in his misfortunes as the angel of the Lord did our first parent, and comfort him in the same words as our immortal poet uses, in a similar situation to that first child of human misery: "Go thy ways in peace, "the world is all before thee, where to seek a place of rest "and providence thy guide."

The singularity of the case before me, and the uncommon hardship the supposed criminal will suffer, if any further

ther ſteps ſhall be taken to urge the vengeance of the houſe againſt them, not only unheard in their own defence, but even uninformed of the charge, induces me to endeavour to draw the attention of the Houſe of Commons, and the public to this extraordinary attempt of the committee.

Between the return of the firſt report, on which the legiſlature had acted, and the introduction of the ſecond, in which the curious inſinuations are preſented for the conſideration of the public. Mr. Philip Francis arrives, who, finding that the Directors of the Eaſt India company treated him as he moſt certainly deſerved, not only for penning his inſolent letter to them at his leaving Bengal, but alſo for his ſending it to be publiſhed in all the daily papers. Full of ſpleen and malice he applies to the committee, ſitting at Weſtminſter, to countenance his abominable falſhoods. Had I been chairman of that committee, moſt certainly I would at leaſt have been neuter in that whole buſineſs. It reſted with him not to engage the paſſions of the awful ſenator, in the paltry politicks of the Eaſt India proprietor. When the devil ſhews his cloven foot, in vain does he attempt to lead us into vice, with the ſyren's ſong or angels face. Let the General harangue to all eternity, not one man will he convince that he is actuated by virtue or from public good in the preſent buſineſs; whether you Sir, are ſubject to the ſame concluſion I ſhall leave others to determine, but I heſitate not one moment to declare that to this cauſe, and to this cauſe alone we owe the reference back, to the former report, for one ſolitary piece of evidence, (extracted, not given) in juſtification of the opinion implied of there having been more of

policy

policy then of justice in the condemnation and execution of Rajah Nundcomar.

I have said a great deal in my former letter to you, Sir, on the *crooked politicks*, and unfounded assertions of this genuine knight of the post, and in some degree I stood pledged to dissect his letter, No. 7, of your Appendix. Indeed I have such a fertile field before me of instances of this gentleman's want of candour and disregard of truth, that I am at a loss from what part of his literary productions to cull my examples.

With your permission, and in order to keep in view a former assertion of mine, viz. that he entered and left Bengal in the same gloomy habit of soul, predicting the sudden and absolute ruin of that kingdom. I will present you with two instances only from the first letter of the majority, to the Court of Directors.

" 37th. Paragraph of a letter from the majority at Bengal, to the Court of Directors, dated the 3d of December, 1774, about six weeks after the arrival of General Clavering, Colonel Monson, and Mr. Francis, at Calcutta.

" On this everlasting theme of Mr. Hastings, we shall " only for the present observe in general, that under any " tolerable form of government the effects of the famine " must long since have ceased to be felt in a country where " nature asks nothing of the governing power but not to " study to resist and defeat her operations. The world " will soon see that it is oppression of the most violent and " pernicious nature, which has reduced this fertile country " to a state of depopulation."

I defy

I defy even you, Sir, who I believe to have read every thing that has ever been written on government and politicks, to produce, collected together in so few words, arguments so foreign to experience to human reason and to truth And introduced for no other purpose, than to lead the mind off from a fact, which nobody can deny, to daring assertions which nobody will believe.

The severity of the famine was felt in the summer of the year 1770, it swept away a full fourth of the labouring people of the provinces of Bengal. The letter from which the above paragraph has been taken, was written in the beginning of December 1774, a little more than four years afterwards.——Mr. Hastings's argument led to prove that one cause of the collections falling short, was the vast number of the cultivators of the lands, (from the crops of which the revenues arise) having been swept away by the famine. If it should please God, in order to punish us for our manifold sins to visit this kingdom, with so dreadful a calamity, as in one summer, to carry off one quarter part of the working people of this country, and the revenues fall short in consequence. Would you, Sir, dare to insult the understanding, and play upon the feelings of the house, by assuring them, that the present evils did not arise from the famine, but intirely from the mismanagement of the former admistration?

If, as they affirm, the government of Bengal had a tendency to the depopulation of this country, how as it came about, that the famine and government together hath not yet quite extirpated the people and destroyed the revenues. Mr. Hastings had been but a little more then two years in the government of Bengal, when the majority arrived, supposing him to have been the whole time employed,

as

as they would have us to believe in devising the means to finish what the famine had begun, two years before he came from Madrass, and laid waste the whole kingdom. If they establish this fact, will it not bare hard on several others of theirs, which may be found on the company's books, from November 1775, to September 1776? When the evils returned with redoubled violence, by the power reverting into the hands of the Governor General, by the death of Colonel Monson.

In the short space of time, which elapsed from the sailing of the last ships in April, 1775, (when they rested their cause on the strength of the accusations, (how collected, I have shewn) and sent home, as being quite sufficient to bring about the recall of Mr. Hastings) to the death of Colonel Monson. Their letters to their honourable masters, the East India company, and to the ministry, took a different turn. They had by their presence restored health, peace and plenty to the country, and liberty to the very few inhabitants they found. "The steady power which "had been employed to resist and defeat nature's "operations." They had effectually removed, and people sprung up together with rice in the fields spontaneously. These poor young naked natives they clothed, the hungry were fed, and the golden age had returned so suddenly, that every body was lost in rapture, and joyous amazement; and all this had been brought about by their having found in themselves those men, "by whose future services, and by "what future exertion of virtue and ability such a state "can be recovered. Common men are not equal to the "occasion."

Unhappy Bengal, what pity that these angelick beings were not of the nature of Swift's struldbuggs, but that on

one

one of them dying, every thing ſhould in the inſtant fall back into its former ruin and deſolation. In ſhort, if you believe your friend Mr. Francis, Caos was come again.

I feel very unhappy that I cannot amuſe myſelf in his golden regions, his ſhort lived elyſium, to converſe a little with his beings, of a ſeaſon which ſprung up with his power, and could not be held back from ſinking again into nothing, on the demiſe of Colonel Monſon, it requires a pen like your own, Sir, to furniſh a proper epitaph on the occaſion.

No one circumſtance of the conduct of Mr. Haſtings in his preceding adminiſtration, was left untouched, all was pointedly condemned and execrated, in ſelect and choſen words and phraſes, in this mine Mr. Francis toiled inceſſantly, as I ſhall abundantly ſhew. Major Scot having trod the ground before, has diſpoſed of the treaty of Benarras, Rohello war, King's tribute, and ſeveral other ſubjects, but the mine is inexhauſtable, and would furniſh endleſs materials to prove that the majority never once expected that their repreſentations would be controverted or their aſſertions diſputed, but depended entirely on the prejudices of the nation and the influence of the miniſtry, to bring about the recall of the Governor-general The following paragraphs have been extracted from one of the firſt letters of the majority to the Court of Directors.

"Paragraph 70. The letters received by General Cla-
"vering from ſeveral of the company's military officers

"entruſted

" entrusted with separate commands, will be found deserv-" ing of notice. They contain accounts of military ex-" peditions and hostilities carried on against a number of " Rajahs and Zemindars, without any authority from the " present government, or any direct communication to us of " the plan of execution of them. Most of these measures " appear to have been directed by the provincial chiefs of " Patna and Burdwan some time after our arrival here.-- " In some places, the Rajahs are reduced to obedience, " and give hostages.——In many others, the villages are " burnt, and the corn cut down and destroyed. Ensign " Scott, having received orders from the Chief of Patna, " to seize or expel Rajah Tuttah Shaw, pursues him into " Sujah Dowlah's dominions, and makes three of the " Vizier's subjects prisoners of war.——Captain Crawford, " by order of the Chief of Burdwan, entered Patcoom " on the 5th of last Month with six companies of Sepoys, " took the capital, levelled the town, and cleared the " country, in order to make the post tenable. On the " 9th, he attacks and drives the natives before him, " after which, *the whole country fled into the mountains.*-- " He says, he is endeavouring to sow dissention among " their Chiefs, so as to induce them to submit, or enable " him with ease to rout them out.

Paragraph 71. " We do not pretend to determine at " present whether measures of this nature be necessary or " not; but, we think it very extraordinary, that military " expeditions of such importance, and leading to such " consequences, should be undertaken, not only without

" the

" the orders, but without the knowledge of this board.--
" We are ſorry to be obliged to conclude this article with
" declaring, that, as far as we are able to judge, the
" general principle which ſeems to have animated this
" government, as well with reſpect to the natives of the
" provinces as to the neighbouring ſtates, has had too
" near a relation to the expreſſive words ſo often made uſe
" of *extirpate*, *exterminate*, *rout out*, and *annihilate*.

(Signed)

J. Clavering.

Geo. Monſon.

P. Francis.

What uncandid miſrepreſentations have we here of neceſſary political meaſures, unavoidable in their nature, except we ſit tamely down whilſt a race of lawleſs ſavage Barbarians lay waſte and depopulate our moſt fertile plains.

Though Clavering was violent, and Monſon ſarcaſtic, they were accompliſhed ſoldiers—and, I hope, ſtrangers to the above deteſtable chicanery, though the language and ſentiments ſuit Francis exactly.

Many parts of the provinces of Bengal and Bahar are bounded by thick woods and hills, riſing one above another to a moderate height——ſeveral of the valleys behind the woods, and between the mountains, are inhabited by different tribes of unſocial beings, not many degrees removed from the ſavage life.———Theſe banditti had, under all governments, in all periods of known

time,

time, infested and laid waste the fertile cultivated plains of the above-mentioned provinces, now possessed by the East India company——Various plans had been formed, and many experiments tried, to reduce these people to order, and to cover the farmers in the adjacent plains from their mischievous devastations; which continually destroyed the inhabitants, and impeded the collections of the revenue.———By degrees, a chain of military posts had been formed on the confines of our territories, which connected with, and supported one another.———The officers commanding these posts were in general put under the directions of the civil servants superintending the collections in the district on which the post depended ——others commanded partizan-corps, stationed in the hills, and acted under the immediate orders of the presidency.———Many of these commands were so distant from Calcutta, that it was indispensably necessary for the board to give general instructions, and confide a great deal in the discretional conduct of the different collecting residents, and commanding officers. The powers of the former were not unsimilar to those anciently given to the Lords of the Marches in England, to repel by force of arms, the sudden incursions of a fierce, valiant, northern people——and the latter had such kind of orders as our modern commanders receive when intrusted by government with an expedition against a neighbouring state.

All that was intended, was the preservation of the lives and properties of the company's farmers, or (if you like it better) the king's subjects.——If this could be be effected by moderate means and fair treaties with the Rajah's, Zemindars, and other Chiefs of the hill-people (as those motley tribes of independant free-booters are commonly called) it was so to be effected--if not--then they were to proceed by force to drive them further from our boundaries, or, if necessary, to subject them entirely to our government.——Look round the world——search into every page of antient and modern history, and inform the public, how a new sovereignty, lately acquired by conquest-part of a vast continent--and in a similar situation with the provinces of Bengal and Bahar——is by other means to be defended and maintained.

But there were orders of the East India company's which positively forbad a further extention of their dominions on that side of India: and it was for the purpose of the majority, that the necessary and unavoidable measures which had been taken in order to form a strong barrier for the safety of those dominions, should be represented in Europe as a breach of those orders, and an avaricious ambition in the late administration to obtain new provinces for the company by the force of their arms.——With what candour, and on what foundation, orders, issued to obtain the very purposes intended by the company, have been perverted by the majority, in order to criminate the conduct of the Governor General, has already been shewn.

Such were the men the late ministry provided to correct abuses, and give to the government of this deluded kingdom, candid information of the real state of the company's affairs

affairs in Afia, and I am much miftaken if the Loid Advocate, in his late much ftudied harangue, has not let puffey peep a little too plainly out of the bag, by giving the houfe to underftand, what the intentions of the laft minifters were with refpect to India affairs, the fending out of another fhip load or two of locufts, under the denomination of fupervifors, to devour the remaining wine and oil of that country (unhappy) Bengal. I will hope that we have efcaped that great evil, and that no more duplicates of coerfive meafures, or Bofton Port bills are to be fent as padlocks on the Ganges, but that the time is arrived when not only the nation, but even the East India company are emancipated from their fervile and dependant fituation, on a venal court faction.

An honourable Baronet complimented the able advocate on his acquiring fuch extenfive knowledge in Afiatic affairs in fo fhort a time. Had he forgot that the man comes from the Northward and was bread a lawyer. What has he collected but words. I will venture to wager with the honourable Baronet, that if he will but fend him or any other famous man of the profeffion, half a peck of Pagados; they will collect much better words, and more of them in his defence. His lordfhip ftrews a few laurels on the grave of that wonderful man Lord Clive, (on whofe vaft abilities I never think but with admiration) but I remember other orators of the fame profeffion ftraining all their powers to blacken the character, and tarnifh the luftre of that great hero's virtues. Is the nation never to allow a little honeft praife to living worthies. Muft no good man tafte of fame

in

in the vale of peace, ſhall ſuch an incendiary as I have and ſhall prove Mr. Francis to be, have his works made part of the national records, and in the ſame volume, a ſtain be thrown on the ſpotleſs character of Governor-general Haſtings. If forgetting the injuries done by the dead; and applauding thoſe now forging by the living is the high road to intereſt in this world, and Heaven in the next. I fear, I ſhall ſtay where I am until the curtain drops, and then ſink into the oppoſite place to Heaven. For I feel no ſymptoms of repentance working on my mind, and people advanced in life do not grow leſs obſtinate by living longer.

Now, Sir, for a fair inveſtigation into the merits of Mr. Francis' letter to the Court of Directors; their neglect of which your committee ſeems ſo extremely diſpleaſed with. I grudge ſuch a document the paper it has already waſted, and is about to waſte; but this man muſt be put totally to ſilence, and the labourers which he keeps about Debret's ſhop, diſmiſſed to ſeek their bread by ſome more worthy employment, then alarming the nation with fictitious accounts of things which never exiſted. Abler workmen have taken the matter up in a much more honourable place, or I ſhould never by ſuch grubs as thoſe have been rouſed from my compleat contempt for them and their maſter.

I have, Sir, cauſed the whole letter, as it ſtands in the Appendix, No. 7, to your report, to be copied in ſeperate paragraphs, and under each paragragh you will find my remarks

remarks and obſervations, this I thought better then being obliged conſtantly to refer the reader back to the letter itſelf. No man knows, Sir, better than you do how neceſſary perſpicuity is to the fully underſtanding what a writer means.

From

FIRST COMMITTEE,

Second Report.

APPENDIX, No. 7.

(COPY.)

Mr. Francis's Letter to the Court of Directors.

' Gentlemen,

' FOR your Convenience, as well as to aſſiſt my own ' Memory, I have thrown together, in the Paper ' which I have now the Honour to deliver you, ſhort Me-' morandums of the principal Points on which I wiſh and ' propoſe to give you all the Information in my Power. ' Some Things will require Explanation—others may have ' been omitted, which I may recollect hereafter. I am ' ready, and ſhall be ſo at all Times, to anſwer any Queſ-' tions you may think fit to put to me; and I hope that, ' if any Thing farther ſhould occur to me, which may eſ-

'cape my Attention, you will allow me to communicate 'it to you in Writing, whether as a Correction of any of 'the Contents of this Paper, or in Addition to them.

I have the Honour to be,

East India House, Gentlemen,

19th Nov. 1781. Your most obedient and

humble Servant,

P. Francis.

REMARK.

Knowing the desponding spirit and aptitude at fiction to which Mr. Francis was so excessively prone, I cannot blame the Court of Directors for being content to hold no farther converse or connection with the man.

'Chairman and Deputy Chairman of the Honourable the 'Court of Directors'.

'East India House, 19th November, 1781.

Par.1. 'When I had the Honour of addressing the Court 'of Directors from St. Helena, it was not known to me, 'that one of the Subjects on which I proposed to give 'them Information would be brought so directly and ex-'plicitly into their View, as I find it has been, by Mr. 'Hastings's Letter to them of the 2d of December, 1780— 'as he therein expresly tells you,' "That they shall be "under the Necessity of making a large Reduction and "possibly a total Suspension of your Investment for the en-"suing Year; and that he cannot pronounce what their "Ability may be, beyond that Period."— 'I have nothing 'to 'to offer on that Head, but that I am thoroughly con-'vinced that the Neceſſity to which Mr. Haſtings alludes 'will continue to operate, if not increaſe, in its Force, 'and in all its Effects; and that no Man, who knows any 'Thing of the real Sate of India, can, even by Conjec-'ture, point out a Period at which ſuch Neceſſity will 'ceaſe to be felt. Peace at preſent is not within Sight; 'and, whenever there ſhall be a Peace, I can venture to aſ-'ſure you, that the comparative State of your Expences 'and Reſources in India, as they will then ſtand, will not 'exhibit a Surplus applicable to the Purchaſe of an In-'veſtment. It is my moſt ſerious Opinion, that you will 'never again have an Inveſtment purchaſed with any Sa-'vings from the Revenues of Bengal. I hear you have lately 'authorized the Governor and Council to draw upon you 'for Five hundred thouſand Pounds, to be applied ſtrictly 'to this Object:—You know, better than I do, how long 'the Company can ſupport ſuch a Demand upon their 'Reſources in England.—As long as it can be ſupported, 'you will conſult the welfare of *Bengal* at leaſt, in lay-'ing this Burden on the Company. If there be no In-'veſtment purchaſed in one Year, the landed Revenue of 'the Country will, in a little Time, be found to fail nearly 'in the ſame Proportion: One is, in effect, the Supply 'of the other.—Again, as there is properly no Trade in 'Bengal, or next to none, but that which is created by the 'Purchaſe of the Company's Inveſtment, it follows, that 'in whatever Proportion ſuch Inveſtment is diminiſhed, 'the Manufactures are ſo far forth left without Employ-'ment—the Conſequence of which muſt be, that they will 'either fly the Country, or turn to ſome other Occupa-

'tion, and the Manufactures be proportionably debased, if 'not irrecoverably lost.—Reflections of this Nature, I 'presume, must have occurred to you, when you autho-'rized the Governor and Council to draw upon you for so 'large a Sum. Whether it will be in their power to apply 'the Whole of it in the Manner you expect, I very much 'doubt:—But as a collateral Resource, applicable to the 'same Object, I submit to you to consider, whether the 'following Idea might not be adopted with Advantage, 'under such Corrections and Improvements as your own 'Judgement may suggest: That all Europeans, and others, 'resident in Bengal, having Money which they wish to re-'mit to England, should be invited to subscribe it into the 'Treasury of the Board of Trade, to be applied to the 'Purchase of Piece Goods, Raw Silk, &c. on Condition 'that their Bills on the Company, at a favourable Rate 'of Exchange, (suppose, for Example, 2s. 1d. the Current 'Rupee,) shall be accepted and paid at a given Period after 'the Arrival of the Ships in England. This Expedient, 'I believe, will produce Twenty-five Lacks a Year, at 'least for a Year or Two; and, as far as it went, the Ex-'traction of Specie from England and from Bengal would 'be proportionably and equally saved. I submit this merely 'as an Hint to your better Judgment.'

REMARK.

Mr. Hastings had some doubts that he should not be able to continue the full support of four different armies, belonging to the Company, then actually in the field, and looking, every man of them, to Bengal for support and subsistance; and at the same time continue to send annually home

home to the Company an investment amounting to eight hundred thousand or a million of pounds sterling, as he had done for years past; besides supplying money and provisions to Bombay and Madrass.——So circumstanced, he thought it his duty to advise the Company at home of his apprehensions, that they might not load themselves with the expence of unnecessary tonnage, in order to carry home Bengal goods which it might happen he could not spare money to provide. —— Was not this justifiable and fair? has such a necessary piece of advice had any bad effects? and has not his powerful and unwearied invention of finding out resources enabled him to go on with the investment? and is it not now known, that there is, at Bengal and on its way home, more than a million and a half of Bengal goods, provided to enable the Company to make good the bills which necessity has obliged the different Presidencies to draw on the Company?

In the latter part of this first paragraph, Mr. Francis modestly offers a hint to the Court of Directors which he would hope to intrude on the world for his own. —— Is it possible that this man was unacquainted with all the different ways that this his hint has been given to the Company before, so far back as to the years 1762 and 1763? I remember Mr. Gregory, now the Chairman of the Court of Directors, (whose honest name I would not presume to join with Mr. Francis, were it not in the cause of truth,) often mentioned his apprehensions, that sending of so much money out of the country as was acquired by individuals, and at the same time their supplying the foreign Companies for bills, which prevented the farther importation of bullion, would in a few years impede

pede the neceſſary circulation in the provinces, and hurt the revenues, wiſhing ſome means could be deviſed to receive private property for notes on the Company. A few years after, Governor Verelſt ſtated this matter fully and fairly to the Company, with his fears of the conſequences, hinting at the ſame remedy. After that, a merchant of extenſive experience ſtated in the Free Merchants Letters the ſame evil, and propoſed the ſame remedy. —— From this laſt Maſter Francis (being very fond of the man) ſtole the hint as he calls it: but he cannot even ſteal fairly. The author of the Free Merchants Letters propoſes that the Company ſhall receive the current rupee at the exchange of two ſhillings, and grant bills on Europe at very long ſight; and Mr. Francis well knows that all the Europeans in Bengal would very gladly pay in every ſixpence they could get on ſuch terms, with a view that they or their friends ſhould receive it in Europe, with an intereſt of three per cent. even five years after paying of it into the Company's caſh at Bengal. —— Had he offered this exchange I ſhould have ſaid nothing: but his cunning (for it is all he has to ſerve him in place of wiſdom) ſuggeſted that, though he himſelf had taken money out of the treaſury for his wages at two ſhillings the current rupee, yet that he never had paid in any at leſs than two ſhillings and one penny; and he thought that, if he gave in his hint on terms leſs advantageous for others than he had taken for himſelf, ſomebody would take notice of it.—— Thus do the wicked ever dig pits for others, and fall into them themſelves: for I dare him to deny that he ever received money from the Company at more than two ſhillings the current rupee, or took bills on them for leſs than two ſhillings and one penny.

‘ The

Par. 2. 'The Second Point, on which I meant to offer 'you some Information, was the State of the Administration 'of Justice in Bengal; but, as I find that this Subject has 'been already taken up by the Legislature, and is likely to 'be resumed at the Meeting of Parliament, I shall not en-'ter further into it in this Place.—One Fact only it is fit 'you should be apprized of, because it directly concerns 'the Company's Interest, and may require some immediate 'Orders from you. It is, that whereas, in many Acts and 'Declarations of the Governor General and Council, and 'more particularly, in their Declaration made to the Su-'preme Court of Judicature on the 11th of March 1780, 'it was constantly avowed and maintained by them, that 'the Zemindars and other Landholders of Bengal were 'exclusively subject to the Jurisdiction of the Governor 'General and Council—the Chief Justice of the Supreme 'Court was nevertheless appointed, in October, 1780, by 'a Majority of the Board, consisting of the Governor Ge-'neral and Sir Eyre Coote, against Mr. Wheler and me, to 'be Superintendant or Judge of the Dewannee Adauluts, 'and to decide, in the last Ressort, in all Appeals from 'those Courts;—that the Chief Justice had accepted the 'Office; and, that on the 24th of October, the Governor 'General proposed an Allowance of 5,600 Sicca Rupees a 'Month for the Chief Justice, which at that Time was 'not voted.'

REMARK.

The subject of appointing the Chief-Justice to the superintendance of the Sudder Dewanne Adaulut, with a salary adequate to the fatigue of the Duty, was proposed as a conciliatory measure, and referred home to the Company for

for their approbation. The reasons for the turn given to it in the Committee have been explained in this and my former Letter. —— I shall only subjoin here, that, though Mr. Hastings has been continued in the government ten years, so oddly have things fallen out, that no plan of his has had any time given it to prove by experience its utility. At Bengal they are now acting under the sanction of the Acts of Parliament of last session, little dreaming that all is going to be new-modelled. — With such unsteadiness of government at the seat of empire, how can we expect tranquillity and ease at the extremes; which, in point of distance by sea, must be considered, with respect to the Mother Country, as antipodical.

Par. 3. 'These Subjects being dismissed, I come to the 'great leading Facts, which constitute the actual State of 'India, as far as I am acquainted with it—1st. The Dominions of your Ally, or rather your Vassal, the Nabob 'of Oude, are utterly, and I believe irrecoverably, ruined. 'In the Year 1776, the Revenues of that Country, and 'its Dependencies, exceeded Three hundred Lacks of 'Rupees. In April, 1780, they were so reduced, that, 'whereas the Company's Demand on the Vizier for that 'Year, as stated by Mr. Charles Purling, amounted to 'One hundred and Twenty Lacks, and, as stated by me, 'to One hundred and Fifty Lacks, no Assignments could 'be had from the Vizier for more than Ninety Lacks, 'and he himself was reduced to the absolute Want of a 'bare Subsistence for himself and his Family. You will 'find the Particulars recorded in our Consultation of the '3d of April 1780. You cannot but be sensible how far 'the Fact of itself extends, and to what Consequences

'it

' it leads. I mention it now for the following Reason, ' out of many that are still more important. I find, that ' in the Report of the Committee of Proprietors, dated ' the 19th of December 1780, Credit is taken (under the ' Head of Outstanding Debts due to the Company) for ' Current Rupees, 25,65,989, due by Asoph ul Dowlah, ' Nabob of Oude, with as much apparent Confidence and ' Security, as if you had the Money in your Treasury in ' Leadenhall-Street:—Now I do assure you, that this ' Debt, so far from being discharged, is by this Time ' immoderately increased; and that it never can be dis- ' charged out of the Revenues of Oude, which, when I ' left India, were far short of being equal to the indis- ' pensable Establishments of that Government, and which ' were still declining rapidly every Day.—2d. I have good ' Reason to believe, that your *Ally*, the Rana of Gobub, ' as I find him entitled in the Governor General's Letter, ' is much dissatisfied with the Presence of your Troops, ' and with the Effects it has produced in his Country: ' That Major Popham was so apprehensive of being be- ' trayed by him to the Marattas, that he seldom or never ' ventured to communicate his Plan of Operations to him, ' and more particularly in the Instance of his Enterprize ' on Guawlior: And that no Part of the Subsidy due by ' the Treaty from the Rana, or only a very small Propor- ' tion of it, had been discharged. The Truth is, he is ' too inconsiderable, that I had hardly ever heard of his ' Name, before the Treaty of Alliance with him, and ' Guarantee of his Dominions, were proposed by the ' Governor General.—3d. With respect to the Rajah of ' Berar, you are already in Possession of my Opinion of

 ' his

'his Views and Disposition towards our Government, and 'of the Intent and Consequence of his keeping an Army 'stationed upon our Frontier in Cuttack. In my Letter 'of the 29th of March last, I told you that he had made 'a Demand of Money from us, for the Payment of this 'Army. I must now add it as a Fact, which I have ab-'solute Reason to believe true, though I am not able to 'prove it, that Money, to the Amount of Three or Four 'Lacks of Rupees, was actually sent to the Commandant 'of that Army, and that a much larger Sum was pro-'mised by the Governor General, without the Advice, 'Consent, or Knowledge, of the Council. With respect 'to the Detachment under the Command of Lieutenant 'Colonel Pearce, avowedly formed for the Purpose of 'marching through Cuttack and the Northern Circars, 'towards the Carnatic, and of co-operating with Sir Eyre 'Coote, I must inform you, that so long as the above 'Maratta Army remains upon our Frontier, the Detach-'ment cannot move without leaving Bengal open to In-'vasion; that, while the Marattas keep the same or any 'other situation upon our Frontier, they necessarily engage 'too much of our Force and Attention from other Ob-'jects; which, without an actual Rupture with us, pro-'duces many other Effects of the most avowed Hostility. 'I do not think the Governor General himself will deem 'it prudent to move Colonel Pearce's Detachment South-'wards, until the Danger, which may and ought to be 'apprehended from the uncertain Motions of the Rajah 'of Berar, shall be clearly and absolutely removed: He 'cannot do it, but in Contradiction to *my* Opinion, re-'peatedly given at the Board, and which ought to hold

'good

'good as long as the State of Facts is the same: He never 'can obtain the Consent of Mr. Wheler, who I know is 'immoveably fixed in this Point: And finally, he cannot 'do it even with the Approbation of Sir Eyre Coote, 'who, though very desirous of receiving every possible 'Support from Bengal, did nevertheless freely admit that 'the Measure was not to be thought of, unless we were 'perfectly secure of the Maratta Army in Cuttack. You 'already know, that, in November 1780, the bonded and 'other Debts against your Treasury in Bengal, exceeded 'Eighty Lack of Current Rupees. You may depend 'upon it, that that Burthen will increase as long at least 'as the War continues, and as long as Money can be 'borrowed on any Terms.—4th. In the Report of the 'Committee of Proprietors, I find the bonded Debt of 'Bombay stated at Bombay Rupees, 35,11,955. The 'Fact is, that, on the 30th of April 1780, their bonded 'Debt amounted to Bombay Rupees, 50,89,213. Having 'no Means to pay the Interest of 9 per Cent. on this 'Debt, their Practice is to convert the Interest at the 'End of every Half Year, into Principal. Supposing this 'to be done, as I have no Doubt it has been, the Result 'will be, that, at the End of October 1781, their bonded 'Debt will amount to Bombay Rupees, 58,07,634, ad- 'mitting that the Debt is not otherwise encreased by an 'additional Loan. It is also a Fact, that, by their own 'Estimate, their Expences from April 1780 to April '1781, would exceed their Resources in the Sum of 'Rupees, 38,34,492, which of course is a Debt on the 'Government, whether bonded or not: The whole Bom- 'bay Debt, therefore, without reckoning any Thing in-

 'curred

'curred since April last, must now stand at Bombay Ru-
'pees, 96,42,126, and this I believe to be very much
'under the Amount.'

REMARK.

The foregoing paragraph runs up to so many counts, as the lawyers call it, that it will be no easy matter to separate them. The first is in the true style of ruin and despondence with which Mr. Francis has at all times exercised his pen.

To this I shall only observe, that Mr. Francis and his friends were in the government of Bengal when the Visier Soujah Dowlah died; persued what measures they pleased as to the mode of conducting the government of his country; for Mr. Bristow, the confidential friend of the majority, a very worthy and capable young man, was sent up as dry-nurse to the foolish fellow and worse than beast, Ausoph ul Dowlah, the Visier's son and successor. Nothing was or could be done, in that government, but by the orders of the majority, recommended and carried into execution by Mr. Bristow. The Idiot-Nabob's army was reformed, his household settled, his civil-list disbursements arranged, and every single circumstance adjusted, by themselves, under management of their own agent, who continued there until the beginning of 1777; when Mr. Middleton, who had been resident at the old Visier's court before their arrival, was sent by Mr. Hastings to supplant Mr. Bristow, as Mr. Bristow had been sent by the majority to supplant him. —— This gentleman, well versed in all the affairs of the visier's court, continued to act about the same length of time as Mr. Bristow had acted, when Sir Eyre Coote, wishing

wishing to have Mr. Purling made the Resident, another very able servant of the Company's, well versed in the languages and modes of conducting business in Asiatic courts, was sent in the room of Mr. Middleton.

Soon after the time this last Gentleman went up, Mr. Francis states the total ruin of the country of Oude, in a style of dependence peculiarly his own. —— Would it not have been candid in him to have said something of the time this great ruin commenced? or does he mean to infer that Oude, like Bengal, during the management of their agent, Mr. Bristow, flourished in all the luxury of plenty; but, the instant Mr. Middleton returned, all was ruined and destroyed? —— I believe the people of this country begin to be a little too well acquainted with his monstrous stories, to believe, on his bare word, that the Visier's dominions, during his and his friends administration, produced full three millions of pounds sterling per annum; but that, in less than three years after his party had lost the power, the Nabob and his family wanted a bare subsistence. Such an assertion is truly worthy one of the disciples of NUNDCOMAR's academy: but that does not lessen the insult offered to the House of Commons and to the nation, for imposing on them such improbable and abominable falsehoods.

2dly. The Rana of Gohud Mr. Francis never heard of before: that, as luck will have it, may be true; his enquiries led him not that way; if they had, he would have heard of that tributary prince and fifty others who inhabit the continent of India: but a man, that should set himself up for a person who understood the politics of of Europe, and at the ſame time own that he never heard of the Prince of Heſſe, the Elector of Hanover, Swiſs Cantons, Republics of Venice, of Florence, and other ſmall States of Italy, would not have much credit given him for his knowledge in the affairs of Europe.

Very numerous are the ſmall States of Aſia, whoſe ſituation obliges them to watch the motions of the great Potentates, and trim over, firſt to one, and then to the other, as intereſt may incline or neceſſity compel. But of this Mr. Francis knows nothing; nor does he ſeem to know, that, ſince the Engliſh have eſtabliſhed themſelves on that peninſula, a kind of balance of power hath imperceptibly formed itſelf, that will, in all human probability, on a general peace taking place, (which we may expect to hear of ſhortly,) be adjuſted in ſuch a manner as to ſecure the tranquillity of that continent for many years to come.

3dly. Whenever Mr. Francis, urging his opinion, depends on his own poſitive aſſertions, he is for ever unluckly. The detachment under Colonel Pearce did move on, and arrived ſafe on the Coaſt. He ſhould be more cautious of committing Mr. Wheler, now he is no longer influenced by his pernicious counſel: that Gentleman is emancipated; and, having had time to think for himſelf, joins the Governor-General in all his plans for a peace; to obtain which honourably, you know, ſir, nations muſt ſhew a power to reſiſt by war.

If Mr. Haſtings did on his own private credit raiſe three or four lacks of rupees, and with ſo ſmall a ſum purchaſe the neutrality of ſo powerful a branch of the Maharatta Empire as the Rajah of Berar, and thereby enable Colonel Pearce

Pearce to pass unmolested through not only his dominions, but also through the dominions of the Soubah of the Decan, and join Sir Eyre Coote on the Coast with such a noble reinforcement,——what words are strong enough in which to speak the praise due to such a noble effort of disinterested patriotism! A Prince nearly connected, by every tie natural and religious, to the first Maharatta Power against whom we were in arms, and himself able to bring forty thousand horse into the field, has been bought off, by Mr. Francis's Account, for thirty or forty thousand pounds.—Cheap doings, these; I wish some of our European politicians could do such jobs so reasonably.

Par. 4. '5th. I cannot speak particularly of the bonded 'Debt at Fort Saint George; but I have heard, from good 'Authority, that it amounted to the utmost they could 'borrow. One Fact, however, is necessary to be brought 'into your immediate Observation; that whereas the 'Committee of Proprietors have taken Credit in their 'Report for out-standing Debts and Property at Fort 'Saint George, convertable into Cash, to the Amount 'of £1,380,083: That whole Credit, or by far the 'greatest Part of it, is ideal. Their Expences are esti'mated by Sir Eyre Coote at above Seven Lacks of Ru'pees a Month, which, he declares, "must *all* come from "Bengal, as there were no Resources in the Carnatic "from which a single Pagoda was to be expected."

REMARK.

The statement of the Debts, due on bond at the different settlements, I shall admit to be accurate, though brought forward by Mr. Francis; and shall only observe, that

that the aggregate sum does not amount to what the Bengal bonded debt alone amounted to when Mr. Hastings came to the Government of that Country.

The annual revenues of Bengal alone amount to more than double the sum; and, if we add that part of the Revenue of Oude which must, and always will, be applied to the payment of our army on the peace establishment, this bugbear of Mr. Francis will disappear insensibly in a year or two after the present troubles subside.—— The Company's bonds, like our national funds, rise or fall in their value on a nearer or more distant prospect of a peace. I have known them formerly often above Par in the market; nor is it ever but with reluctance that the Bond-holders at Bengal bring them in for payment; and the Government may always reduce the interest to five per cent. which is not equivalent to more than two per cent. in Europe.

Par. 5. '6th. In Bengal, I am first to observe to you, that ' all the Establishments in the Civil Departments have ' been immoderately increased since Sir John Clavering's ' Death; but these, however great in themselves, are not ' to be mentioned in Comparison with the Excess to ' which the Military Charges have been carried in the ' same Period. In the 28th Article of the Instructions ' which General Clavering, Colonel Monson, and I, car- ' ried out with us, in the Year 1774, the Company say, " Our Military Expences at Bengal having increased to " a Degree which is become *insupportable* to us; we, in " an especial Manner, enjoin you to make strict Enquiry " into the Causes of such Increase, &c." At that Time, ' the Military Charge, which the Company called *insup-* ' *portable*,

'*portable*, as in Truth it was, did not exceed Eighty
'Lacks of Current Rupees per Annum; the Estimate of
'the same Establishment, for the Year ending in April
'last, amounted to Two hundred and Fourteen Lacks
'and an Half; and this Charge, I conclude, has in-
'creased in the current Year; I am sure it cannot have
'been diminished. I am unwilling to say any thing of
'the actual State of the Army, in regard to its effective
'Strength, compared with the Establishment, its Disci-
'pline, or the Punctuality with which the Native Troops
'are paid, because it would be going out of my own
'Department, and partly because I cannot give you
'Lights on this Subject, from my own direct Knowledge
'of it: Thus far, however, I think it my Duty to say,
'that from my own Observation, and from all the Infor-
'mation I have been able to collect, I have too much
'Reason to believe, that your Army actually wants a
'strict Inspection into its Discipline, and a vigorous
'Command over it; and that this is true in a Degree
'much beyond what you will be inclined to believe, or
'what I could make good. The Thing in its Nature is
'not capable of Proof in England; your Judgement there-
'fore must be guided and determined by your Opinion of
'the Veracity and Honour of those whom you consult.'

REMARK.

Mr. Francis would certainly have done wisely in saying nothing about the army, even on his own principles, his extreme ignorance on the subject: but there are other more weighty reasons, which having slipped his memory, I shall take the liberty to recal them to it.

At what perlod did this want of order and diſcipline commence? did it exiſt when General Clavering arrived in the country? if ſo, how came it to paſs that that Gentleman during his life never ſaw the Bengal Army? His military pride would not ſuffer him to let Colonel Monſon have the command of it until he himſelf ſhould get into the Government. Was it of more conſequence to the State and to the Company, that he ſhould ſpend his time at Calcutta, endeavouring, by means ſhocking to think on, to drive Mr. Haſtings out of the Government? When have the Bengal Army refuſed to do their duty? Are not their warlike exploits and military prowеſs the theme of every man in Europe and in Aſia? Has there been a time when they ſlunk back from the charge, or rather did not court the occaſion to be led up to the noſes of thirty times their numbers, arranged in military array, hoſtile to the Engliſh banner? Where were the feelings of the *would-be-patriot* General, when he ſuffered ſuch a Thing as Mr. Francis to caſt ſuch a reflection on the Bengal Army? Is this his mode of paying his court to a ſet of as brave officers as the world ever ſaw? — But they have done with Mr. Francis, and I truſt will no more be in the way to be inſulted by the General's inſolence of manners: being ſecured from that is all they have to aſk; their real contempt for ſuch aſſociates will do the reſt.

General Sir Eyre Coote was the immediate ſucceſſor appointed by the King and the Company to command the Aſiatic Troops in general, and the Bengal Army in particular. Has that gallant Officer made any complaint of the want of ſpirit, order, or diſcipline, which he found in the Company's Troops? Has he not, with a mere handful

of

of them, chastised the Cesar of the East, or rather parliamentary bugbear, Hyder Ally? But it is not in the nature of a certain order of men to forgive a political sin. Sir Eyre voted against Mr. Francis in council, and that is a crime of such a dye as no length of time will wash out. I hope the Bengal officers, now in England, will signify their thanks to this clerk of the war-office for his opinion of them.

' 7th. In the Report of the Committee of Proprietors,
' I am sorry to observe, among several other exceptionable
' Articles, that Credit is taken for Outstanding Debts,
' due to the Company in Bengal, to the Amount of
' Current Rupees 77,22,548, and that this Sum makes
' Part of the final Balance of Pounds Sterling, supposed
' to be in Favour of the Company, just as much as the
' Money in your Treasury, or the Value of the Goods in
' your Warehouses, in London. I beg Leave to assure
' you, that these Debts, or the greatest Part of them, have
' stood for Years on the Company's Books, and are be-
' lieved in Bengal to be desperate. I declare to you I
' never heard of a Debt of any Consequence being re-
' covered by the Company in India. If *these* Debts were
' of a recoverable Nature, it is to be presumed that a con-
' siderable, or at least some, Part of them, would have been
' recovered at a Time when the Governor-General and
' Council were trying every possible Expedient to borrow
' Money at an high Interest: But the Fact, on the con-
' trary, from a Comparison of the Accounts in my Pos-
' session, stands thus:

 ' 25th

'25th September 1779, Total Debts due to the Company, — —	108,21,543
'31st October 1780, Ditto, —	110,74,218
'Increase of Debts due to the Company in those Thirteen Months,	2,52,675

REMARK.

Of the outstanding debts, on the desperate situation of which Mr. Francis expresses himself so feelingly, it is no less curious to observe his ignorance than to remark his malice. Outstanding debts, he says himself, are very seldom recovered in India, and gives an instance to prove that they increase yearly. Is it possible that this man can be ignorant, that, in the complicated character in which the Company stand of Lord Paramount, Farmers General, Collectors of the Revenue, Import and Export Merchants, and Military Store-keepers General, all which accounts pass their mercantile books, and must be productive of bad debts: is there any thing new in this? are they not obliged every year to write out to their servants at their several settlements, to write off to profit and loss such and such desperate debts? Had he been the least conversant in the Company's mercantile affairs, he could not have been ignorant of this fact; and that the servants abroad never do proceed to strike any head off their books without express orders from home. And, since they have been so deeply concerned in the politics of Asia, many millions have sunk that way, and more must be sunk every year; but the observation served to catch the eye of ignorance, and to give alarm, and that was all Mr. Francis meant;

meant: candid disquisition, or honest explanation he has always been a stranger to.

'8th, Thus far, without descending to minuter Objects, I have confined myself to what I believe to be, strictly the Facts, in stating to you the general Situation of your Affairs: My Opinion on some of them shall be laid before you, with the same Freedom and Sincerity.

'I find, with Concern, that a Habit begins to prevail in this Country, of sending out new Corps of Europeans for the Service in India. In my Judgement, and in that of all the Officers of Experience with whom I have conversed in Bengal, you would find it a much less expensive and a much more effectual Method of providing for that Branch of your Service, if you sent out Recruits sufficient to complete the European Regiments at the several Presidencies. The dividing those Regiments into Two Battalions each, when the Companies could not shew above Twenty-three Rank and File, was a most ill-advised Measure, and produced many bad Effects, besides a very great Increase of Expence. When I left India, they wanted more than Half their Complement. Your Army in Bengal, if the Establishment be kept complete, is sufficiently numerous; it does not want Field Officers, at least not many; nor Captains, nor Subalterns; in these Ranks, I believe your Army is as well supplied as any Service in that Country can require: But it does want Two or Three General Officers, Men of Activity, of Experience, and of established Reputations; if possible, they should be in the Prime of Life, and as high in Point of personal Rank

'as

'as can be found; under *their* Inſpections, your Eſta-'
'bliſhments will be kept complete, and your Troops in'
'general acquire as much Diſcipline and Vigour as an'
'Indian Army is capable of, or as the Nature of that'
'Service is likely to demand.'

REMARK.

Here we have him again in the field, confeſſedly out of his element. Have the officers trained up in the Company's ſervice ſhewn any want of ability, when they had, by riſing gradually, come to the command of the army? Will he be content to abide by the event of every experiment which has yet been tried, and contraſt General Clavering, General Monro, General Stuard, Colonel Leſley, Colonel Edgerton, with Lord Clive, General Joe Smith, General Caillaud, General Sir Robert Fletcher, General Sir Robert Barker, and General Thomas Goddard? I drop the General of the Committee, for fear of hurting his modeſty, not well knowing in which liſt he would like beſt to be placed.

I am neither civilian nor ſoldier in the Company's ſervice; but am extremely hurt at obſerving the temper with which the Gentlemen, who fall under thoſe deſcriptions of Company's Servants, bear to be ſo groſsly inſulted, in the face of the Nation, by ſuch a botch, ſuch a carbuncle, on the vitals of Truth, as this quondam clerk of an office, whoſe ſoul has been ſhrivelled up like a winter's pippin, and compreſſed, by the dirty employ of ſtopping ſixpences, into the magnitude of a minikin pin's head.

'9th. With respect to your Connections or Differences with the Country Powers, I have already told you in what Estimation the English Name and Authority are universally held by those Powers. The Re-establishment of Peace in India, which in Effect is no more than reverting to your own original Principles, is now become indispensably necessary, not only to your Prosperity or to your Safety, but I say to your Existence. If the present Wars are to be continued, you can no more support the Consequences of Success than of Defeat: No Victory in India will ever again pay the Expence of the Army that gains it. I need not tell you, what effect another Defeat might produce. The Disaster which besel Colonel Bailie's Detachment, was felt in the most distant Parts of our Provinces: Another Event of the same Nature would, as I apprehend, go near to drive all the Sepoys out of your Service. — Before the late unfortunate Transactions on the Two Coasts, the Reputation of your Arms had supported your Credit and Influence throughout India. But that Reputation has been wantonly hazarded and severely wounded; and your Credit and Influence have accordingly sunk along with it. Peace then, at all Events, must be your Object. On this Point I can give you other Explanations, if they are desired; if not, I shall content myself with saying, that the Indian Powers have lost all Confidence in the Good Faith and Steadiness of the Government of Bengal.'

REMARK.

We know, Mr. Francis, that you have, over and over again, told the Company and the Kingdom at large many most daring and fallacious stories of the estimation in which the

the English name is held by the different powers of Asia,— and I wonder that, as you must have taken your account from some interested Agent, it has not happened in one single instance that the man's own interest should operate so as to instruct you in a little truth.

The disaster which befel the little gallant body of men under the command of that excellent Officer, Colonel Bailie, was brought about by the (what shall I say) great Generalship of one of those kind of Officers of which you want to add a few more to the Company's troops— The defeat of the Bombay army happened whilst another of those heroes commanded it —— but perhaps more immediately by that absurd policy which put the Civilian's coat so improperly on the military shoulders of General Clavering, and sunk poor Carnac from an excellent Officer into a field Committee-man. When you say that the country powers have lost all confidence in the good faith of the Government of Bengal, you should in justice have told us, that such want of confidence was never known before you and your colleagues arrived at Bengal, and that we removed it as soon as it was known that you had left it.— I instance that you have been so unlucky as to risque your whole credit upon the marching of Colonel Pearce's detachment through the dominions of the Rajah of Berar, of whose hostile intentions towards the English you have told such dismal stories; through the Soubah of the Decan's dominions, and the territories of his brother, with half a dozen other independent Rajahs and Zemindars, all of whom furnished him and his army on their march with every thing their country produced: which circumstance gives

gives the direct denial to your gloomy predictions of the inimical disposition of the country powers to the English —And the repeated successes of our arms, under Coote, Carnac, Goddard, Popham, and several others, are such examples of the recovery of the credit of our military character in Asia, that I wonder the news of it has not induced you to go hang yourself.—This preservation of you, I suppose, we owe to the fostering care of the General of the Committee; who, rather than not try the experiment of revenging himself on those whom he deemed his enemies, would embark his small stock of credit in partnership with such an adventurer as Mr. Francis.

Par. 9. 'You cannot but be thoroughly possessed of my 'Opinion of the Injustice and Imprudence of all our Pro-'ceedings with respect to the Marrattas: On this Subject 'you *now* have all the Evidence before you, that Argument '*and* Reason, confirmed by the most ruinous Experience, are 'capable of furnishing. In attempting to support the Pre-'tensions of Ragoba, and the Views of the Presidency of 'Bombay, you found the *unanimous* Opinion of the Go-'vernor General and Council, that is, of Men who sel-'dom agreed in other Points, decidedly against the Mea-'sure. This was true at least in the Year 1775, though 'a different System has since prevailed in Bengal. I shall 'say nothing of the Conduct of Mr. Hastings's Negotia-'tion with Moodajee Boosla. You see to what a State 'they have reduced us, and in what Conclusion they 'have ended. In my Judgment, the Principle, on 'which that Scheme was professedly founded, stood in 'Opposition to the obvious dictates of sound Policy and 'common Sense. After the Death of Madharow in 1772,

' the Union of that great Body, which constituted the ' Maratta Empire, was dissolved. The principal Chiefs ' set up for themselves, and no longer acknowledged any ' one common Superior; or, if they acknowledged the Su- ' periority of the Infant Peshwa, it was purely a Matter of ' Form. In this State, they naturally endeavoured to se- ' cure their respective Independence, by courting the ' Friendship, or at least by avoiding the Enmity, of the ' English Power. In what Sense could it possibly be our ' interest to restore the Union of an Empire so dissolved, ' supposing the Attempt practicable, or to vest its united ' Strength in the Hands of a single Person? In the Year ' 1778, they were so divided among themselves, that no- ' thing but our invading their Country, with the avowed ' Design of overturning their Government, could have ' made them act together. — Such was the Plan of Mr. ' Hastings's proposed Alliance with the Rajah of Berar, as ' it stands exhibited in his Instructions to the late Mr. ' Elliot, in July 1778, and in many other recorded Docu- ' ments. The same Plan included another Object, not ' less unwise in Point of Policy, and still more dangerous ' in the Execution than the first: I mean the Project of ' uniting with Moodajee Boosla, to invade the Dominions ' of Nizam Ally Khan, and to deprive him of a considerable ' Part of his Possessions. From this Project, which could ' not be long a Secret to the Nizam, the subsequent Union, ' which appears to have been concerted by him, between ' Hyder Ally, the Marrattas, Moodajee Booslah, and him- ' self, took its Origin. The Invasion and Ruin of the ' Carnatic sprung from the same Source; and, in Conclu- ' sion, the Rajah of Berar, for whose Advancement the Plan

' is

'is professedly formed, joins in the Confederacy against 'us, and in Effect (though not yet avowedly when I left 'India) becomes one of the most dangerous Enemies we 'have to contend with. If this Confederacy should not 'be strong enough to maintain itself, and to accomplish 'the Designs of the Contracting Parties, whatever they 'may be, their last Resource will unquestionably be, to 'call in the French to their Assistance.—I will not tres-'pass, Gentlemen, any longer on your Patience.—If Ob-'jections are made to any thing advanced in this Paper, I 'believe I can answer them. If Explanations are wanted, 'I am ready to give them.—In entering so far as I have 'done into such a Detail, it is not my Purpose to criminate 'any Man, nor even to condemn Measures, merely for the 'Sake of condemning them.—Your Governments in 'India are actually involved in a Labyrinth of Difficulties. 'I therefore think it my Duty to trace to you the principal 'Steps by which you have been, imperceptibly to your-'selves, misled into this Labyrinth; because I believe it to 'be the surest, if not the only Method you can take, to 'find you Way out of it.

P. Francis.'

REMARK.

I come now to the last paragraph of this famous letter, and I do assure you, Right Honourable Sir, that I am very glad of it; for, to labour through such a collection of dismal prophecies, unsupported assertions, and positive falshoods, without one ray of truth on which to rest the mind for a moment on the way, is, as you will know, no easy task.—The hodge podge complexion of this take-leave paragraph is ſo perplexed, from containing the eſſence of all the foregoing ones, that I ſhall limit my remarks on it to a ſingle obſervation, or at moſt two.

In this part of his letter, Mr. Francis in ſome degree acquits Mr. Haſtings of being the original cauſe of the Maharatta war. His reaſons are obvious enough;—becauſe, another Committee from your Houſe having the matter before them, it was more his immediate intereſt to ſpeak truth than otherwiſe. But what will he ſay to his Agent Mac Intoſh, whom he diſpatched home the ſeaſon before he came himſelf with frightful accounts of the Maharratta wars, Rohillo wars, and cargoes of other falſehoods againſt the Governor General, all which was iſſued out of his mint in Piccadilly. If he does not getſomething done to ſtop the mouth of that ſable, predatory hiſtorian, he will moſt aſſuredly turn his black gooſe quill againſt his maſter; for he is one of thoſe Swiſs-like penmen, who will undertake any cauſe; and if I had any uſe for pamplet-manufactures, I would certainly buy him over with the other half-crown.

Mr. Francis declares that he does not wiſh to criminate any man; all he means is, that, as the Company's Affairs have been ſo twiſted and twirled, interwoven and knotted together, in which unlucky ſituation he both found them, on his arrival in India, and left them when he came away, he cannot help offering his ſervice to the Company and to Parliament, to endeavour to ſet them to rights again. Whether the experience the Company have already had of his ſervices will induce them to truſt their Affairs again in his hand, I do not know; or whether you, Sir, and his Majeſty's new Miniſters, have in contemplation to cram him,

him, with others of his tribe, down the throats of the Company, as your predeceſſors in office did, you can beſt tell; but I know, that, if the preſent Proprietors of ſtock, and Directors of the Company, ſubmit to ſwallow ſuch a miniſterial potion, I much queſtion whether their conſtitution is now ſufficiently ſtrong to get the better of the poiſonous effects of it; — becauſe I ſuppoſe no man will expect their great Phyſician, Governor General Haſtings, will preſcribe for another ſeven years together the neceſſary antidotes to counteract its pernicious conſequences.

I ſuppoſe, Sir, by your exhibiting of Mr. Francis's productions in the Report of the Committee, that you thought that you had an intelligent, a candid, and an honeſt, man, to deal with, and that you thereby was about to do a public benefit to ſociety: I hope the clear and fair account which I have given you, attended by proofs in almoſt every Page, of his real conduct and character during his ſtay in India and ſince his arrival in England, will have weight enough with you to ſuſpend your final judgment until he has fairly and honeſtly refuted the aſſertions and facts in this and my former letter.

I return with no ſmall degree of reluctance to the part you have yourſelf taken in the compilation of the Report. That you had compiled it from the minutes of the Committee was one of the points in my former letter which I did not preſs ſo cloſely as I ſhould have done had I then had ſo good authority for ſo doing as I have now. Your Chairman, Sir, has paid you ſome handſome compliments on the elegance of the performance, and the information

you

you helped him to; and you, in your turn, rubbed down your honourable Chairman on his great induſtry and abilities.——This, Sir, with great patriots, is very well; and hungry coffee-houſe politicians ſwallow down the condeſcending complaiſance of the two great men, and approve, in ſenators, what, amongſt honeſt tradeſmen, ſuch as themſelves, they would call the moſt fulſome flattery. —— I, Sir, have read both your Reports, over and over again, with an eye to the diſcovery of truth, however it might be enveloped by eloquence; and I am bold again to declare, in the face of the whole kingdom, that, when you penned the reflections and inſinuations quoted in my former Letter, from page 49 of your laſt Report, you had not truth for your landmark. Captain Cowe is the only one perſon, in ſeven very intelligent and very honourable witneſſes, who ſpeaks the leaſt word about its being the opinion of ſome people that the execution of the Rajah NUNDCOMAR was a political meaſure; nor would his ſaying ſo have been admitted as evidence in any other place. The words, Sir, were not his own: they had been put into his mouth by the perſon who examined him; yet, dreadful to think of, this *no Evidence* has induced you to throw out the moſt ſevere and cruel aſperſions on the characters of his Majeſty's Judges and the Governor-General of Bengal. If aſſerting what I feel to be truth ſhall be conſtrued into Scandalum magnatum, call me and try me on the merits: I ſhall be nothing backward to appear.

I am, Right Honourable Sir,
With all due Reſpect,
Your moſt obedient Servant,

Borough, Apr. 18, 1782.

The AUTHOR.

POSTSCRIPT.

POSTSCRIPT.

What a world is this we live in: I can boaſt ſome friends, and to thoſe friends I muſt ſeriouſly appeal, to know, if they think that I have an enemy in the world, who has been made ſo, by any other means than a ſtrong habit of ſpeaking and writing truths, which wound the ear of ſome notorious culprit or public peculator; yet theſe friends write me, in terms rather too harſh for friendſhip, that, by meddling at all in this buſineſs, I have hurt the political intereſts of Governor Haſtings. I never once thought of the Governor: I honour the private virtues of the man; and obſerving, that ſcandal had made its way into the Senate Houſe, where his moral character lay ſtretched on the rack, ready to be offered up, to glut the revenge of men, who hate him for his virtues and his abilities, it broke in upon my reſt, and I ruſhed forward, (perhaps with too little ceremony) to ward the blow, or break its violence; for which, if I am deſerted by thoſe I eſteem.—I ſay with Pope,

Welcome for thee, fair Virtue, all the paſt:
For thee, fair Virtue, welcome even the laſt.

THE END.

www.ingramcontent.com/pod-product-compliance
Lightning Source LLC
Chambersburg PA
CBHW031800090426
42739CB00008B/1089
* 9 7 8 3 3 3 7 1 5 0 4 4 0 *